How to Draw
FACES

Barbara Soloff Levy

DOVER PUBLICATIONS, INC.
Mineola, New York

Note

This how-to book contains a variety of faces for you to draw, thirty in all. You can see that it doesn't take that many lines to create a picture that really does look like a person!

Before you begin your drawing, you may want to trace the steps of each picture, just to get a feel for drawing. Then you can begin to make your drawing using a pencil with an eraser. Each page in the book begins with a picture [top left] of the basic shape of the head. The proportion of the parts of the human face (the relation of each part to the others) is roughly as follows: Divide the face in half from top to bottom and you have the position of the eyes; halfway down from the eyes is the nose; and halfway down from the nose is the mouth. To help you place the eyes, nose, mouth, and ears correctly as you draw, there are horizontal lines across the face. Add these lines in pencil to the face. You can then go on to the second picture [top right] and see where the features should be placed. Add them to your drawing. Then fill in more details when you get to the third picture on the page [bottom left]. At this stage, you can erase the guidelines. Finally, follow the fourth picture [bottom right] to finish your drawing. Accessories such as eyeglasses and hats or caps will be added at this point.

If you are not pleased with your drawing, you may keep working at it, erasing and then drawing new lines. When you are satisfied with the results, you can go over the lines with felt-tip pens or colored pencils. You will be amazed to see that you have produced a very realistic drawing of an individual! You can then color in the drawing with crayons or colored pencils.

Copyright

Copyright © 2003 by Barbara Soloff Levy
All rights reserved.

Bibliographical Note

How to Draw Faces is a new work, first published by Dover Publications, Inc., in 2003.

International Standard Book Number

ISBN-13: 978-0-486-42901-4
ISBN-10: 0-486-42901-6

Manufactured in the United States by Courier Corporation
42901607
www.doverpublications.com

How to Draw
FACES

Practice Page

Practice Page

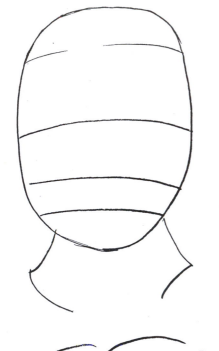

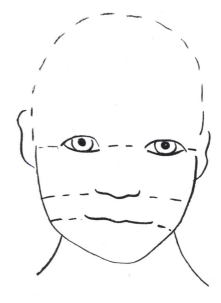

Practice Page

Practice Page

Practice Page

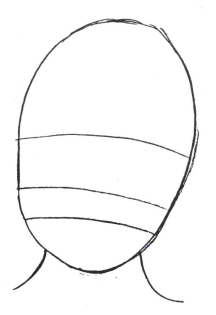

Practice Page

Practice Page

Practice Page

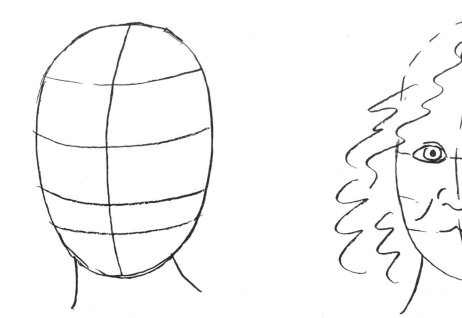

Practice Page

Practice Page

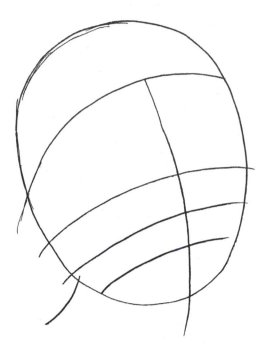

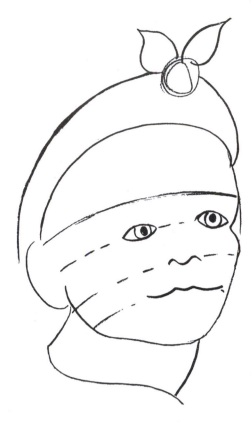

Practice Page

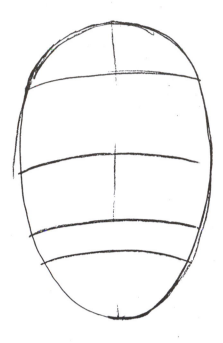

Practice Page

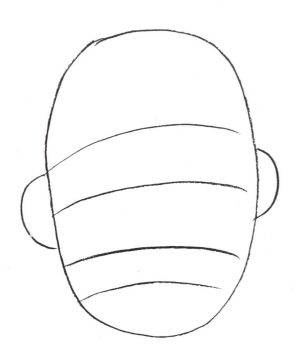

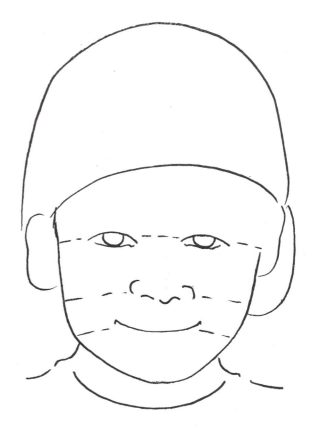

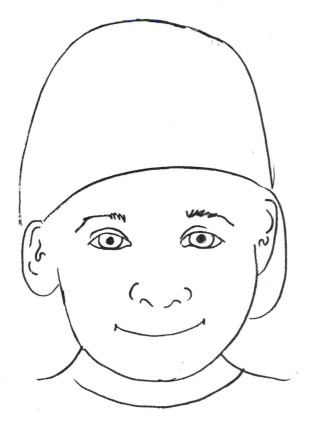

Practice Page

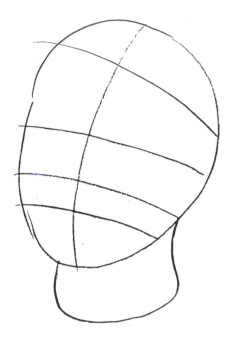

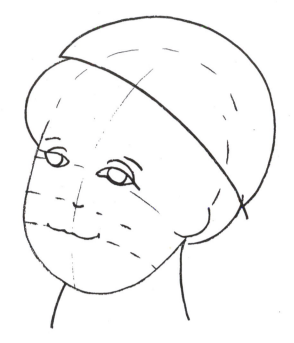

Practice Page

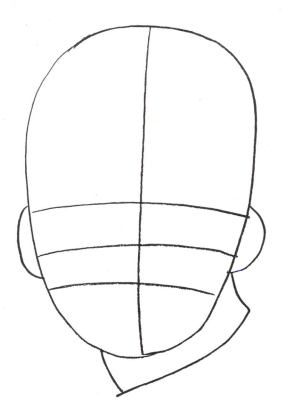

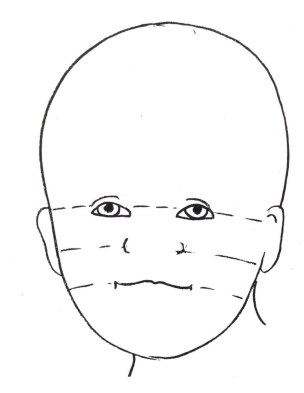

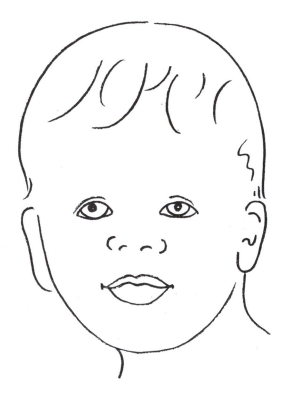

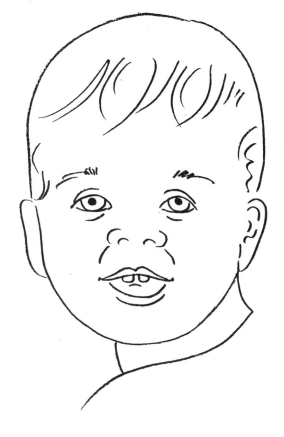

Practice Page

Practice Page

Practice Page

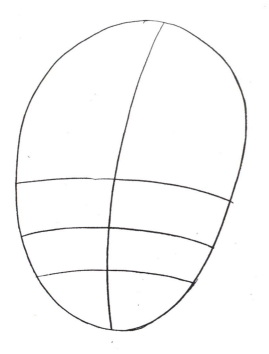

Practice Page

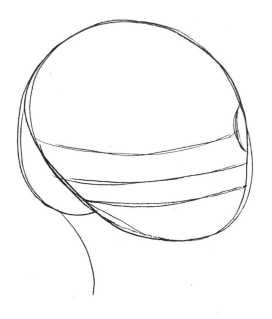

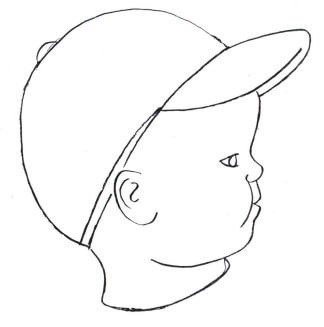

Practice Page

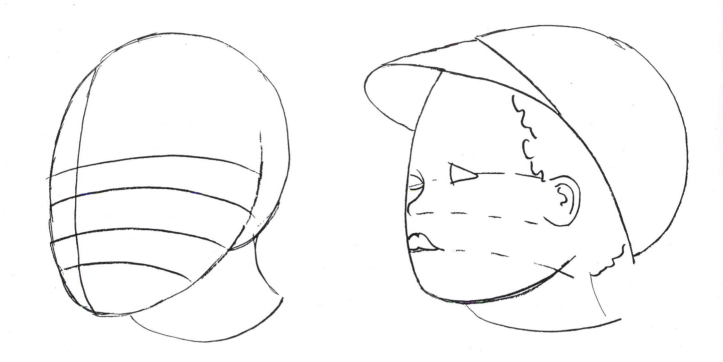

Practice Page

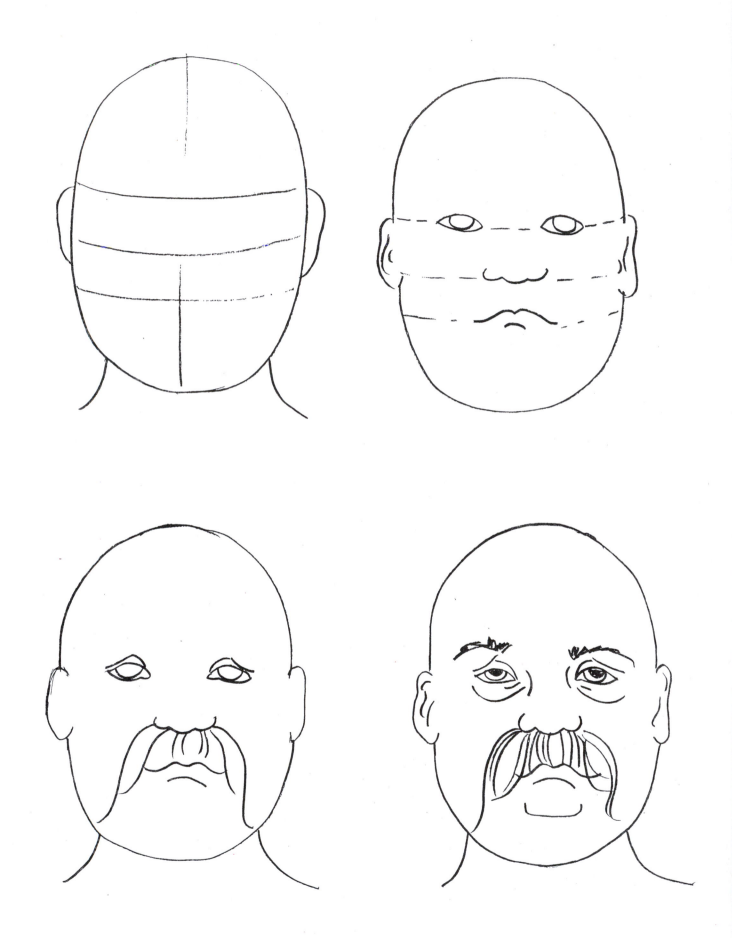

Practice Page

Practice Page

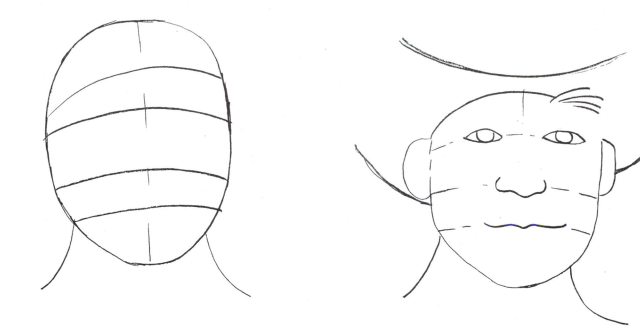

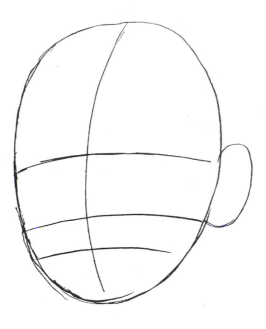

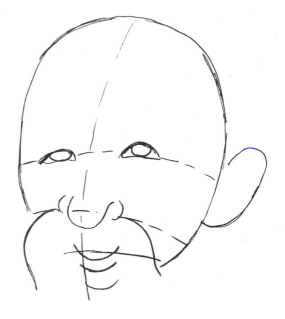

Practice Page

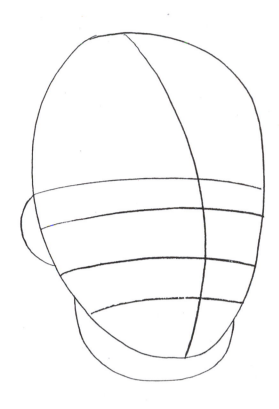

Practice Page

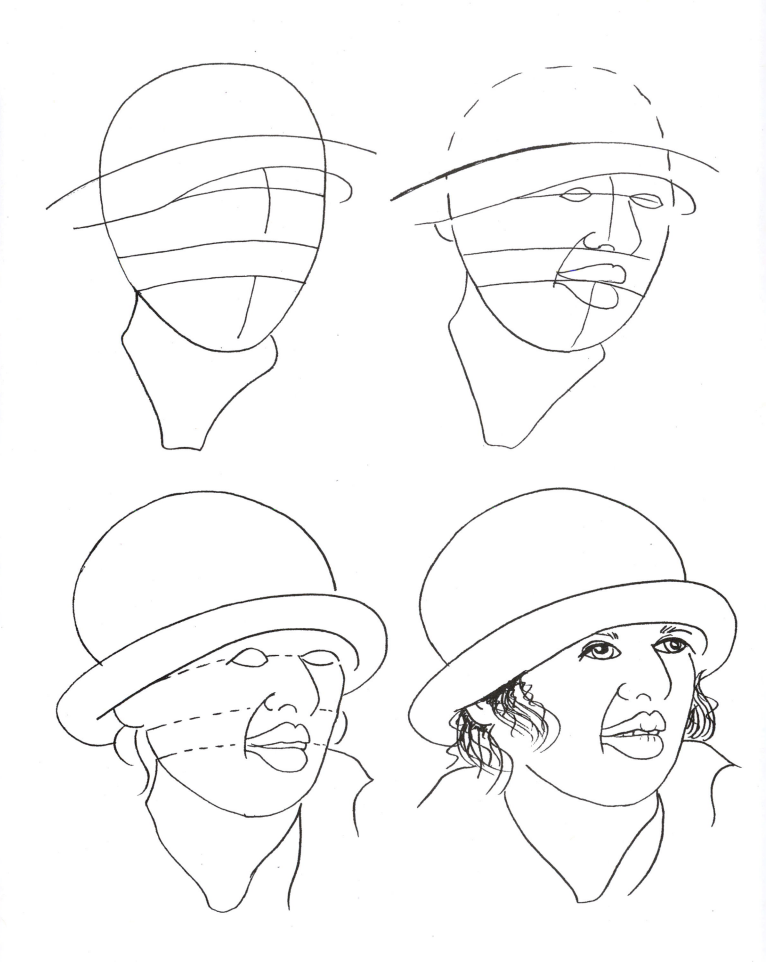

Practice Page

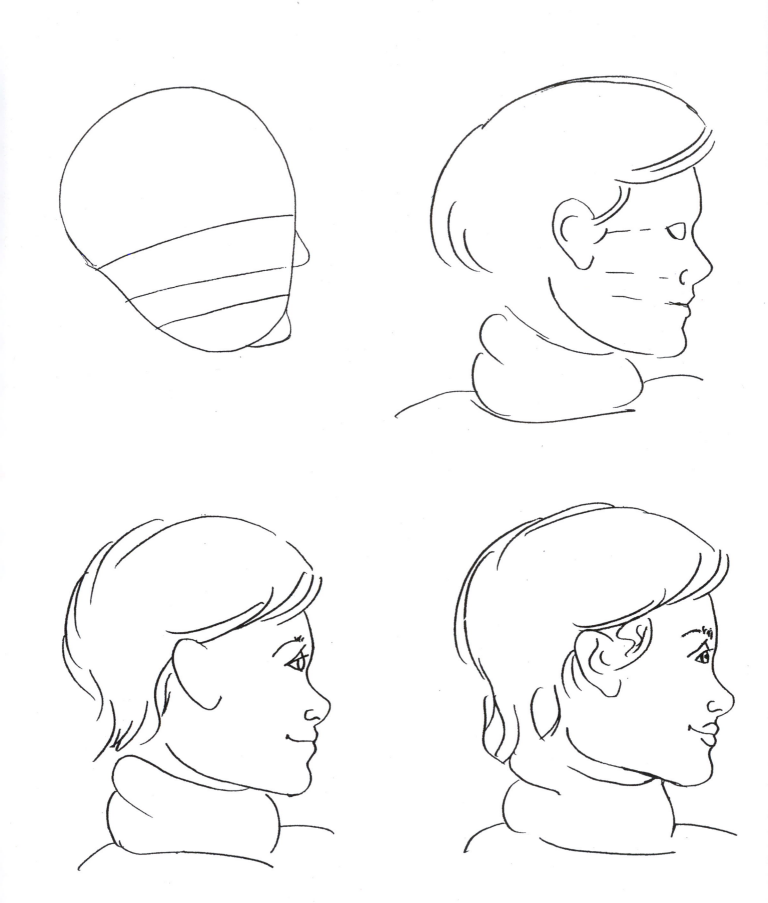

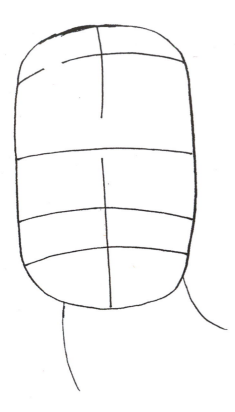

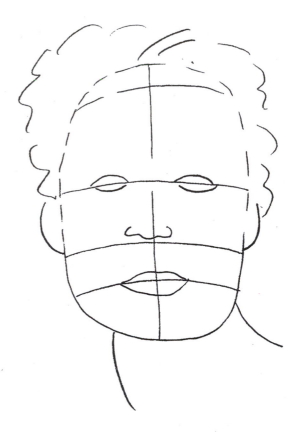

Practice Page

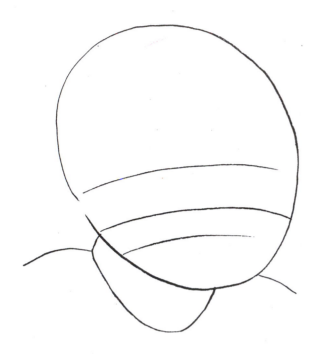

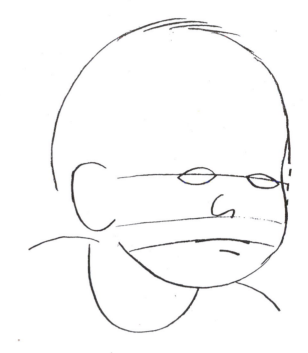

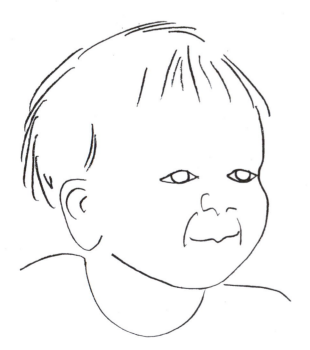

Practice Page

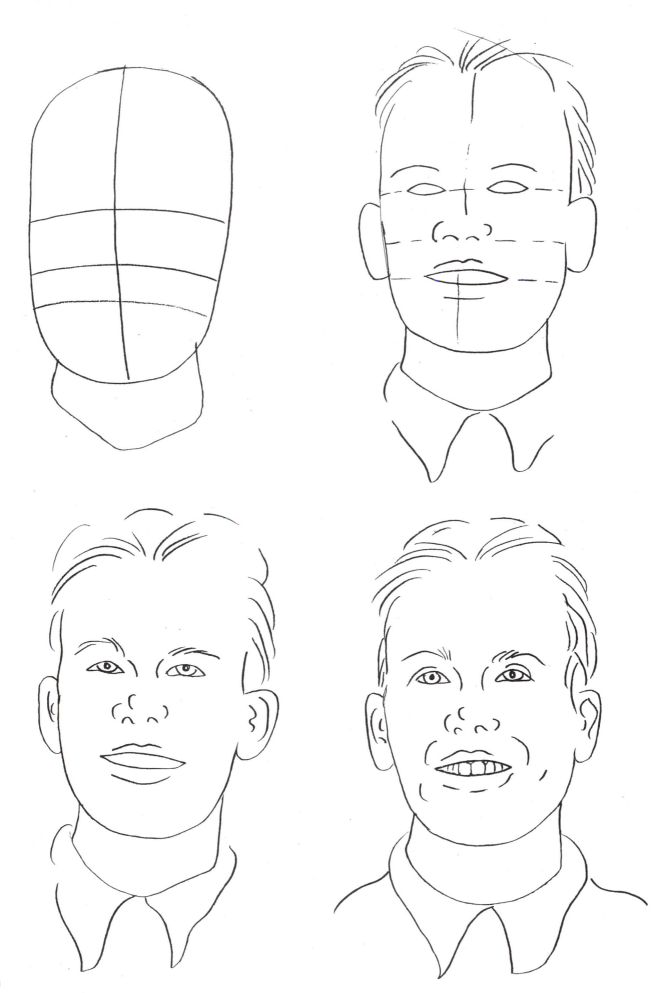

Practice Page